Wolvesey in 1769, looking north-west towards the cathedral across the city wall and the baroque palace. (Painting by John Lewis, reproduced by permission of the Warden and Fellows of Winchester College)

absence of pre-Norman buildings anywhere else below the later palace shows that the Anglo-Saxon palace lay mostly to the north of the Norman palace and must have been extensively destroyed by the moat which once ran along the north front of the twelfth-century palace.

The Anglo-Saxon buildings may have remained standing when William Giffard built his hall to the south west about 1110 and even when Henry of Blois added his hall to the east between c.1135 and 1138, but they will not have survived the

linking of the two halls and the formation of the north front of the Norman palace in the years between c.1138 and 1141.

The Norman palace

William Giffard and the West Hall

William Giffard, the second Norman bishop (1107–29), although nominated in 1100, was not consecrated until 1107. It was perhaps shortly after this that he ordered the construction at Wolvesey of the stone residence now known as the West Hall. This lay south-west of the Anglo-Saxon structures and was not aligned on them, but rather on the boundaries of the ploughed fields which lay to the south. It is attributed to William Giffard partly because its ashlar-work is quite finely jointed and comparable to that of the cathedral tower rebuilt after 1107, and partly on archaeological grounds.

Giffard was a man of great prestige who had been chancellor to William Rufus from 1093–4 until the king's death in 1100, and had continued in office for the first year of Henry I's reign. The residence he built at Wolvesey reflected his status and the wealth of his see (Period I, c.1110). An ashlar-cased structure of flint and mortar on a foundation-raft of timber, measuring overall some 164 feet (50 m) from north to south and 80 feet (24.4 m) in width, it is the largest known non-monastic domestic structure of its date in England, exceeded only by Westminster Hall. Although it is now customary to call such a building a hall, it was in fact a carefully planned block comprising a number of chambers designed to accommodate the bishop's private apartments, a function it continued to serve until the seventeenth century. It did not include a true hall (*aula*) in the sense of the principal apartment of a medieval residence, and this suggests that the Anglo-Saxon hall remained in use. The Anglo-Saxon chapel may also have been retained, for Giffard's structure seems only to have included a small private chapel. Fresh water was brought in by a pipe to a point just outside the north-east corner of the new block. At this stage the pipe-trench skirted the boundary ditch of the Anglo-Saxon palace, a further indication that it remained in use beside Giffard's new building.

Henry of Blois

Nine months after Giffard's death in 1129, Henry of Blois was consecrated bishop of Winchester. He was to rule the see for 42 years, dying in August 1171 in his palace at Wolvesey. By then the house of which he rather than Giffard was the true creator had reached its greatest extent and almost its final form. Subsequent centuries were to witness, apart from the remodelling of Henry's East Hall and of the private apartments in Giffard's West Hall, little more than repairs and occasional modifications.

Henry was a grandson of William the Conqueror and son of Stephen, count of Blois and Chartres (d.1102). He was a monk at Cluny in Burgundy before becoming abbot of Glastonbury in 1126. He continued to hold the abbey when appointed bishop of Winchester in 1129 and came to the forefront of national affairs when his brother Stephen became king in 1135. Henry was not only his brother's chief agent, but from 1136 was paramount in the English church, as administrator of the vacant primatial office (1136–8), and then as papal legate (1139–43). He remained exceptionally powerful until Stephen's death in 1154, but was in exile at Cluny during the first years of Henry II's reign. He returned in 1158 and passed the last thirteen years of his life in the role, as David Knowles put

An English ⌗ Heritage Handbook

Wolvesey

The Old Bishop's Palace, Winchester

Hampshire

MARTIN BIDDLE   MA, FBA, FSA, FRHistS

Director of the Winchester Research Unit

LONDON : HISTORIC BUILDINGS AND
MONUMENTS COMMISSION FOR ENGLAND

Contents

© *Copyright Historic Buildings and Monuments Commission for England 1986*
First published by HBMCE 1986

Printed in England for HMSO by BPCC Graphics Ltd.
Dd 8820915 C90 3/86
ISBN 1 85074 107 7

History

During the Middle Ages Winchester was the richest of the English sees, and its bishops holders of the highest offices in the kingdom as in the church. Two cardinals, two papal legates, a chief justiciar, two keepers of the privy seal, four treasurers, and ten chancellors of England were chosen from their number and since 1348 each successive bishop has been Prelate of the Garter.

Their see was likewise remarkable. Equal in extent at the time of its foundation in 662 to the kingdom of Wessex then expanding rapidly into the West Country, the see was gradually reduced by the foundation of new bishoprics, but by the end of the twelfth century still comprised Surrey, Hampshire, and the Isle of Wight. This vast territory remained unaltered (except for the inclusion of the Channel Islands in 1569) until 1927. In that year the see, 'reaching from the banks of the Thames to within sight of the coast of France', was split into three by the formation of the bishoprics of Guildford and Portsmouth, leaving the greater part of Hampshire and the Channel Islands to form the present diocese of Winchester.

The estates of the bishopric were concentrated in Hampshire, but extended into Oxfordshire, the Isle of Wight, Surrey and Somerset, reflecting the original extent of the see. By the time of Henry of Blois (bishop, 1129–71) these lands were administered from eight principal locations. There were six castles: at Farnham in Surrey, Downton in Wiltshire, Taunton in Somerset, and at Merdon, Waltham and Winchester in Hampshire; and two palaces: at Southwark just to the west of London Bridge and at Wolvesey, in the south-east corner of the Roman walled city of Winchester. Farnham, Taunton and Wolvesey remain in use, but only Wolvesey, after just a thousand years, is still the residence of the bishops of Winchester.

The palace and the city

From 670 the succession of the bishops of Winchester is unbroken down to the present holder of the see. For the first three centuries the bishop and his *familia* of associates and assistants formed the community of the cathedral church. After 963–4, however, when Aethelwold (bishop, 963–84) reformed the three Winchester monasteries, bringing them strictly under the Benedictine Rule, the accommodation at Old Minster – as the cathedral church was by then known – soon proved impracticable and unsuitable. Aethelwold, like many of his successors, was a great figure in the wider world, whose duties as bishop, lord of great estates, and courtier, required an entourage and a flexibility of movement quite alien to the enclosed life of a monastery.

Between 975 and 979 Aethelwold completed his reorganisation of the Old Minster precinct. As part of this process he built a wall which formed the western boundary of an enclosure which was to form the precinct of the bishop's residence. The southern and eastern sides of this enclosure were formed by the Roman city wall, the maintenance of which where it forms the boundary of Wolvesey has ever since been the responsibility of the bishop. The HERRINGBONE *(see Glossary)* flintwork visible on both faces of the wall shows that repairs were already being carried out here in the eleventh century, if not before. To the north the enclosure was completed by a boundary which followed the southern limits of the Anglo-Saxon monastery known as Nunnaminster. The present wall on this line was built in 1377–8.

These boundaries enclosed an area of some 8.6 acres (3.6 ha) which by the thirteenth century was consistently described as *Wulveseye*, 'Wulf's island', a name which presumably refers to the possession by one Wulf of a piece of higher ground between the streams in the valley floor, which became the site of the palace. Excavation has shown that the whole area of the later palace was laid out as water-meadows in the earlier Anglo-Saxon period and that by the tenth century it had long been under the plough. It was thus open ground when Aethelwold enclosed the area in the late 970s.

The royal palace further west, the three great minsters – Old Minster, New Minster and Nunnaminster – and the bishop's palace of Wolvesey formed one of the greatest of all early medieval royal and ecclesiastical complexes. Here in a literal quarter of the walled area of Winchester arose the first great ceremonial centre of the Anglo-Saxon state, the first place to be in some sense the capital of a unified kingdom. The importance which this conferred on the bishops of Winchester was reflected not only in their exceptional abilities as men and as churchmen and in their great landed wealth, but also in the grandeur of their house at Wolvesey which became and remained throughout the Middle Ages their principal residence.

The Anglo-Saxon palace

Very little is known of the palace before the twelfth century. By about 1000 it included at least a hall, the bishop's sleeping chamber, and perhaps a prison. Excavations below the north range of the Norman palace (Rooms 7, 8, 9, 10, 11 and 12) revealed an 'oval' building, some 37 feet (11.3m) long, perhaps a chapel, with western and eastern apses and an added eastern rectangular 'chancel'. The line of this structure was continued eastwards by a range of timber buildings and was bounded to the south and west by a broad shallow ditch, too slight for defence, which perhaps defined and drained the area. The line of the ditch (below Rooms 4, 15, 16, 19 and 18) and the

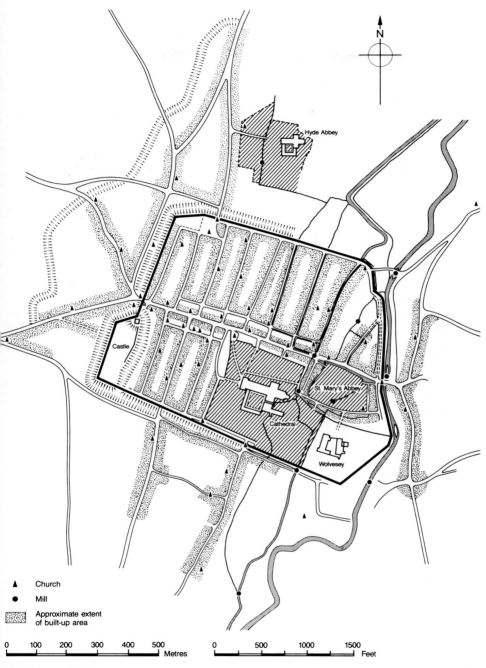

N

Hyde Abbey

Castle

St. Mary's Abbey

Cathedral

Wolvesey

▲ Church
● Mill
▦ Approximate extent
of built-up area

0 100 200 300 400 500
Metres

0 500 1000 1500
Feet

Winchester c.1148

7

it, of a respected 'elder statesman, the father of the hierarchy' (Knowles, 1951).

Henry was a man of exceptional administrative ability and wealthier, so it was said, than any of the magnates or bishops of England. He was a man of taste, a patron of letters and of the arts of illumination, enamelling, jewellery, and goldwork, a collector of classical statues, 'the first amateur of art of his age'. His greatest artistic achievements were his buildings: not only at Glastonbury, Winchester cathedral, the Hospital of St Cross, and Cluny, but also his own houses and castles, 'wonderful structures, gorgeous palaces, huge ponds, difficult aqueducts, and hidden passages in different places' (*opera mira, palatia sumptuosissima, stagna grandia, ductus aquarum difficiles, hypogeosque varia per loca meatus*), as Gerald the Welshman described them. Almost in the shadow of his cathedral, in the city which was until his latter years still

Two sculptured fragments in Caenstone, recovered during excavation. Above: *The decoration of this jamb, probably from Henry of Blois' grand porch added c.1135–8, recalls the facade of Abbot Suger's great church at St Denis, near Paris, consecrated in 1140. Some of Bishop Henry's other sculptures, including the head (right),* echo *this famous work. The figure holding back the hair of this head has been compared to the works of the Master of the Leaping Figures in the great Winchester Bible, illuminated for the cathedral in the time of Henry of Blois*

the centre of royal administration, Wolvesey was Henry's principal seat. The scale and complexity of its buildings reflect his exceptional resources, remarkable activity, and constant interest. Such a house is a mirror to its creator. In the career of Henry of Winchester lies the key to the understanding of Wolvesey.

The building of the East Hall
Henry's first actions at Wolvesey were to relay the lead water-pipe in a stone CULVERT and to construct a new well-house (Period II, c.1130). About the same time he seems to have added a large chapel at right-angles to the south end of Giffard's building. On architectural and archaeological evidence alone one cannot be absolutely certain that these works were carried out by Henry rather than his predecessor. Giffard had ample time to make these changes himself, but the sense of new initiative which they imply suggests that Bishop Henry was their author.

His next move (Period III, c.1135–8) was to construct a second great block to the east, separated from his predecessor's residence by an open space varying between 80 and 100 feet (24.4 and 30.5 m) in width. Unlike the West Hall, this new block was a true hall, a place of gathering, not merely for feeding and sleeping large numbers of retainers, but for meetings and ceremonial. Now known as the East Hall, it contained a hall 88 feet (26.8 m) in length and 29 feet (8.8 m) wide, rising the height of the building. To the south an integral block of chambers rose through two

storeys, and down the west side ran a gallery and porch 136 feet (41.5 m) long, looking on to the space between the two buildings.

Henry may have felt the need for so great a new hall of public audience after his brother's accession to the throne in 1135 and his own appointment as administrator of the vacant archiepiscopal see the following year. The East Hall was clearly designed for synodal and conciliar meetings, like the bishop's hall in Rheims, or that built in Laon early in the twelfth century or in Paris in the 1160s. During Henry's years as papal legate, three legatine councils were held in Winchester, in 1139, in 1141, and in 1143. It seems likely that these were all held in the new hall at Wolvesey.

In the initial stages of building the East Hall, Henry extended the pipeline south to end in a second well-house and pond south of the new hall. It was perhaps at this time that he added a magnificent porch (Room 14) to the north-east corner of Giffard's block. This porch was built of Caenstone from Normandy, although Henry's other buildings at Wolvesey, like those of Giffard and the cathedral itself, were built of Quarr stone from the Isle of Wight. These years probably also saw the final demolition of the Anglo-Saxon palace: Henry's new chapel and hall removed the need for their predecessors, and his hall extended north over the Anglo-Saxon ditch virtually up to the range of timber buildings within this former boundary.

The East Hall was probably complete by 1138 for in that year the Winchester Annals record that 'Bishop Henry built a house like a palace (*domum quasi palatium*) and a strong tower in Winchester'. No one has ever doubted that *domus quasi palatium* refers to Wolvesey, but it is only in recent years that the strong tower (*turris fortissima*), which we would call a keep, has been identified with the site of the former royal palace west of the cathedral rather than with Wolvesey itself.

Civil war

Events in the kingdom in the next years moved rapidly into civil war and later works at Wolvesey can be linked closely both to the conflict and to Henry's role in it. Following Stephen's capture by the Empress Matilda's forces at Lincoln on 2 February 1141, Henry deserted his brother's cause, surrendering Winchester to the Empress with the royal castle, the crown and what little remained in the treasury. On 3 March he received her in his cathedral and the citizens saluted her. A month later Henry secured Matilda's election as lady – preparatory to her consecration as queen – at a legatine council probably held in his new hall at Wolvesey. The Londoners, however, opposed her; Henry was unable to secure her consecration; and alienated by her high-handed actions, both in secular and church affairs, he left her court. Matilda moved with her forces back to Winchester, entered the royal castle, and summoned Henry to her. Returning the ambiguous message *Ego parabo me* ('I will get myself ready'), Henry garrisoned his castle in the centre of the city, and presumably his house at Wolvesey, and left the city to secure the help of Stephen's queen and supporters.

The course of the fighting in August and September 1141, which led to Matilda's flight and the capture of many of her supporters, cannot be followed here. A contemporary, perhaps Robert, bishop of Bath, a close associate of Henry of Blois, makes it clear that Henry had two bases in Winchester, a castle (*castellum*) and a house (*domus*) and that the latter, which can only be Wolvesey, had been strengthened so that it was now impregnable like a castle (*ad instar castelli fortiter et inexpugnabiliter firmarat*). These words imply that the West and East Halls had been joined into a single defensive perimeter (Period IV, c.1138–41) by the construction of curtain walls between them to the north and south of what now became the central courtyard. These works also included the addition of a large latrine block (on the scale of a monastic REREDORTER) to the north end of the West Hall, and the enclosure of a considerable area south of the East Hall. Here a new well-house was built and the pipeline was extended again to feed yet another new well-house built into the new curtain wall to the east. As part of these works of defence the house was now probably moated for the first time.

Almost immediately there were further additions. Unlike their predecessors, these incorporated re-used material (Period V, c.1141). A garderobe (latrine) turret was built against the curtain wall at the south-east corner of the East Hall, probably replacing a wooden structure, since an earlier wall passage led this way from the first floor of the chamber block. A massive wall was also built from the south-west corner of the East Hall towards the West Hall, providing an inner line of defence. Whether these works were built before or after the crisis of 1141 cannot be known, but their materials probably came either from the demolition of the Anglo-Saxon episcopal palace or from another source which must now be considered.

On 2 August 1141, at the height of the fighting, Bishop Henry's forces burnt the city, including the royal palace and its hall. The burning, which may well have been exaggerated, was caused by fire-brands launched from the bishop's keep, now believed to have stood somewhere within the precinct of the royal palace. It can only have been after this that Henry, as Gerald the Welshman records, demolished the royal palace to its foundations, 'suddenly and in haste. . . and in abuse of his public authority', alleging that it was inconveniently close to the cathedral, and carried away the materials to build an outstanding episcopal residence in Winchester.

This must refer, not to the original construction of Norman Wolvesey which made no use of old materials, but rather to the great additions and alterations which now followed (Period VI, c.1141–54), in which re-used stones are a striking feature. Whether Henry's immediately preceding works (Period V), which also used old materials, should be referred to an early stage in this next period we cannot tell, for those fairly limited works may have made use of materials from the older bishop's palace on the site.

Henry's new works were now concentrated on the east side of the palace, making it seem much stronger while in practice greatly improving its amenity. A large square structure, keep-like in plan and external appearance, was built against the east side of the East Hall. It was apparently intended from the beginning to serve as a kitchen (Rooms 23–5). The garderobe turret at the south-east corner of the East Hall was transformed into a massively strong fortified tower (later known as Wymond's Tower). The courtyard south of the East Hall was subdivided

Water-leaf capital of Purbeck marble from one of Henry of Blois' later buildings at Wolvesey. (Courtauld Institute of Art)

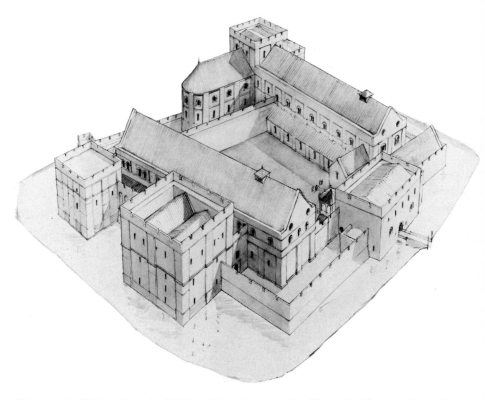

Wolvesey in 1171 at the end of Bishop Henry's reign, with Wymond's Tower and the 'keep' to the left, Woodman's Gate to the right, and the East and West Halls beyond. Reconstruction, looking south-west, by Terry Ball (HBMCE)

and a gatehouse (Room 35) set within it to control access from the reduced courtyard (Courtyard 34) to the entrances in the south end of the East Hall. At the same time the East Hall was raised a storey in height. This gave a third floor in the chamber block (Rooms 28, 29 and 47), and a much heightened roof in the hall itself (Room 19), which was now lighted from three sides by clerestory windows and overlooked from north and east by a galleried passage passing across the windows within the thickness of the walls.

These works may not be strictly contemporary, although the heightening of the hall was certainly related both to the remodelling of the garderobe turret and to the works in the southern courtyard. The blind pointed arches inserted to support the extra thickness of the upper part of the north wall of the hall probably indicate a date towards 1150, but it seems likely that the whole was

Left: *The north-east angle of the East Hall, showing the gallery passage and ball-ornament, looking north-east (Conway Library, Courtauld Institute of Art).* Right: *The north-east angle of the East Hall in 1797, drawn by Sir Robert Ker Porter, showing the return passage along the east wall, to the right (British Library)*

finished before 1154 when Bishop Henry went to Cluny in exile. The following year Henry's castles were slighted, but this seems not to have affected Wolvesey and the recorded payment of £6 12s. for slighting his castle or castles in Hampshire probably refers either to his keep at the old royal palace, or to Merdon, or even to Bishop's Waltham.

Bishop Henry's later years
Bishop Henry returned from exile in 1158 to spend the last thirteen years of his life in England. No written sources reveal the course of his building works during this period,

but it probably saw the addition of a new curtain wall enclosing a narrow courtyard (Rooms 18, 11 and 12) running from the 'keep' around the north end of the East Hall to end in a new gatehouse, later known as Woodman's Gate (Period VII, c.1158–71). This gate (Rooms 3–8, with 2 and 9) seems designed to be the principal entrance to the palace, although it looks north, into the city, rather than south, where the arrangement of Courtyard 34, Gatehouse 35 and the south wall of the East Hall suggests that the main approach may previously have lain. Woodman's Gate projects forward of

13

Woodman's Gate in ruins looking north, by C F Porden, from the title page of Charles Ball's An Historical Account of Winchester with Descriptive Walk *(1818)*

the adjacent curtains, which it commands by flanking loops. Although the outer arch is round, the rear arch of the entrance (Room 5) is pointed and this seems to be a structural rather than a decorative feature. In addition, the east wall of Room 18 abuts on to the north wall of the earlier 'keep' (Period VI). These points all suggest that the construction of the north range and gatehouse belongs to the latter part of Henry's career, after his return from exile and before his death in 1171.

Wolvesey in the later middle ages

The house which Bishop Henry left to his successors consisted of four ranges grouped around a central courtyard, 'well towered and. . . watered about', as John Leland noted four centuries later. It comprised at least thirty-eight rooms on the ground floor, together with six internal courts. From 1262 until the mid-sixteenth century the repairs and alterations undertaken each year were entered on to the Pipe Rolls of the bishopric, a series of annual accounts for all the bishop's manors which runs from 1208–9 to 1710–11. The rolls (in book-form after 1453–4) only survive for 198 of the 283 years during which work at Wolvesey was entered on them, but even so they provide information which is perhaps unparalleled for a non-royal building.

Despite the immense amount of work needed to keep so large a complex even fitfully maintained, the rolls show that later bishops did little to change Bishop Henry's house. This conclusion is fully corroborated by the architectural and archaeological evidence: the ensuing five centuries did no more than add 16 rooms to the ground floor, mostly by subdivision or by encroachment on to the courts. Changes to the upper levels may, by contrast, have been considerable, and the whole house was probably re-glazed and re-roofed on several occasions, and to a great extent re-windowed at least once. Nevertheless, Bishop Henry's house lasted in essence for five hundred years and it is the ruins of his work, and not those of later additions or alterations, which comprise the bulk of the complex today.

There was a great deal more to Wolvesey in the later Middle Ages than can be appreciated today. To the south lay a second court containing stables, barns, a great wool house, the bishop's prison, and an outer gate opening south through the city wall. This considerable establishment reflects the role of Wolvesey as the centre of the bishopric estates. Wolvesey alone of the bishop's seven houses had an exchequer as well as a treasury; accounts were rendered there annually by all the other estates; and the bishop's wool was sent there each year. This pattern was established by the time of the first surviving Pipe Roll in 1208–9 and may have originated, like the Pipe Rolls themselves, in the time of Henry of Blois.

The thirteenth and early fourteenth centuries
The history of Wolvesey during the later Middle Ages can only be traced briefly here. In 1216 the palace was captured by Louis, son of Philip II of France, and the magnates in rebellion against John, but the following year it was recaptured. The bishop of Winchester at this time, Peter des Roches (bishop, 1205–38), played an important role during the minority of Henry III, and the king spent eighteen Christmases in Winchester during his long reign. It was probably during Bishop Peter's time that the East Hall was entirely remodelled (Period VIII, c.1235; but see below, p.35) by the insertion of an arcade between the hall and the western gallery, and by sub-division of that gallery to give the usual later medieval arrangement of three entrances, to buttery, central passage, and pantry, at the south end of the hall. To the south, a cloister-like passage was added across the south side of the courtyard. The buttresses added to the west side of the hall indicate that the windows were entirely remade and the whole effect was probably intended to duplicate as far as possible the design and style of the new hall in the royal castle, which had been finished partly under Bishop Peter's administrative supervision in the years up to 1235. Henry III clearly knew Wolvesey well, for in 1242 writing from Bordeaux he ordered that images in paintings of the Old and New Testaments to be done in the chapel at Windsor should be like those painted at Wolvesey. This order probably refers to paintings undertaken for Peter des Roches – a reminder of an aspect of the palace, along with the painted windows, of which nothing now

Wolvesey and Winchester College c.1736. *Detail from* The East Prospect of the City of Winchester *by the Buck brothers*

remains except for a few excavated fragments.

In the summer of 1258 and again in 1265 Wolvesey came near to siege during the troubles between Henry III and his barons, but when the city was captured by Simon de Montfort the younger in July 1265 the Pipe Rolls comment only that the income to Wolvesey was small because Simon's army had consumed and taken off the corn.

Very little is known of Wolvesey for the next century. Edward I stayed there in 1306, when the bishop's rooms were prepared for Queen Margaret to bear their third child, the royal apartments in the castle having been burnt out four years before. Queen Isabella was there in 1310, and Edward III and Queen Philippa were at Wolvesey for the parliament held in Winchester during March 1330. Repairs went on continuously throughout these years: a new exchequer was built in 1330-1; the great hall (ie the East Hall) and cloister were repaired in 1340-1; and the wool house was rebuilt in 1356-7 (Period IX). In 1347 an iron chain

The medieval and baroque palaces, with Winchester College, founded in 1382, in the background (Copyright Winchester Excavations Committee 1966)

and three bushels of barley were bought for the care and feeding of the bishop's bear after the enthronement of William Edendon (bishop, 1346–66).

William of Wykeham: the palace renewed

The appointment of William of Wykeham (bishop, 1367–1404) marked a new period in the life of the palace. Wykeham had risen in the royal service as he had risen in the church and amongst his successive posts held the clerkship of the works at Windsor (1356–61) before becoming keeper of the privy seal (1363–7) and chancellor (1367-71, 1389–91). His experience in the works led him to take informed action for the care of his houses and the evidence for Wolvesey shows that he acted decisively (Period X).

Early in 1372, the executors of William Edendon finally settled the debts arising from the dilapidations of the castles and manors of the see which they openly admitted were in bad repair. Almost immediately supplies were stockpiled at Wolvesey and the following year, 1372–3, saw the second largest annual expenditure recorded in any of the surviving Pipe Rolls (£199 10s 9½d). The moat on three sides of the palace was widened and deepened; a new curtain wall was constructed between Wymond's Tower and the great kitchen or 'keep', to form the east side of Courtyard 26; a new SALSARY was built in the kitchen; and a new bridge and drawbridge were constructed across the ditch outside Woodman's Gate. The chief work, however, was the complete remodelling of the bishop's apartments in the great tower at the south end of the West Hall, a project which continued for the next four years, and which in 1372–3 alone cost twice as much as the widening and deepening of the moat.

The following year only half as much was spent. The work probably included the building of the curtain wall running north-westward from the corner of the 'keep' or great kitchen, mirroring the wall built the previous year south of the 'keep', and the construction of Room 12, against the north end of the East Hall, as a ground-level wine cellar. Room 15 was built to link the East and West Hall across the north side of the courtyard, and the well-house in the courtyard was rebuilt on a smaller scale. The palace was also thoroughly cleansed; the accumulated floors and occupation débris of the previous two centuries were dug away, often down to the level of the top of Henry of Blois' foundations.

As the pace of work on the domestic accommodation slackened, Wykeham's staff turned their attention to the outer wall of the Wolvesey precinct, which to the south and east was the city wall itself. In 1374–5 and in 1381 this stretch of the city wall was fully repaired and re-crenellated at a cost of over £43. In 1377 a new wall was built to form the north side of the precinct and this wall still forms the boundary against the gardens of the houses on the south side of Colebrook Street. These works were undertaken at a time when invasion was a reality: there were French landings in the summer of 1377 and in 1377–8 Durngate, one of the city gates, was blocked for nine months for fear of the French.

Wykeham's expenditure on regular maintenance never again approached the scale of these early years, but he was usually at Wolvesey once or twice a year, sometimes more often, and between 1374 and his death in 1404 managed to spend at least sixteen Easters there, presumably to celebrate the feast in his cathedral church. Richard II stayed at Wolvesey for the Winchester parliament early in 1393 and the following September he and Queen Anne were probably lodged at Wolvesey when the bishop entertained them to two great feasts. The detailed expenditures for these have survived: £10 1s 2d for 210 guests on Tuesday 16 September; £39 15s 3d for 367 guests the next day; on a normal day at Wolvesey the bishop's household expenses were between £2 and £3. Henry IV stayed here in July 1401, and on 7 February 1403, when he married Joan of Navarre in the cathedral, they were lodged at Wolvesey. It was at Wolvesey too, it seems, that a great feast was held on 5 February, at a cost of £522 12s, to celebrate their meeting: the delicacies included cygnets, capons, venison with furmenty, griskins, rabbits, bitterns, pullets, partridges, woodcock, plover, quail, snipe, fieldfares, roast kid, custards, fritters, creams of almonds, pears in syrup, and 'subtleties with crowns and eagles'.

The fifteenth century

Wykeham died on 27 September 1404, after a reign of thirty-seven years. His successors, Henry, Cardinal Beaufort (bishop 1405–47) and William Waynflete (bishop 1447–86), reigned forty-two and thirty-nine years respectively, so that the see had only three holders in 119 years. Wolvesey was kept in constant repair and major works were undertaken from time to time (Period XI). The north cloister walk (Room 15) was winched upright and provided with buttresses in 1432–3, and the roof of the great hall (Rooms 16, 17 and 19), after giving trouble for years, was completely replaced in 1441–2 at a cost of nearly £300. Beaufort's expenditure for this year, which included rebuilding the pantry, came to £332 0s 7d, the largest sum recorded in any of the surviving annual Pipe Rolls. The rolls for the next four and a half years are missing, a particular misfortune, since it may have been at this time that the chapel (Room 64) was rebuilt, a work which is not otherwise recorded.

Beaufort died at Wolvesey on 11 April 1447. His retirement to Wolvesey, at the end of a long and exceedingly busy public career, may have been the reason for the refurbishing of the great hall in 1441–2, and could well have led to the rebuilding of the chapel in the following years. Certainly, when some of the chapel windows were repaired in the 1470s, the description given agrees with their present arrangement.

Henry VI secured the election of his friend William Waynflete to the see within a week of Beaufort's death. Waynflete made great use of his houses outside London, especially Bishop's Waltham and Wolvesey. At Wolvesey his works (Period XII) cost nearly as much each year as his predecessor's but they have a more intensively domestic character, the result of constant use. The garden in the central courtyard (Courtyard 50) and the private garden ('Rooms' 38 and 43), known as the Queen's Garden, beside the bishop's chamber, are now mentioned frequently for the first time. A new PASTRY HOUSE was built in 1452-3, when the north-west area (Rooms 13-15, 40 and 41) was also reworked; the house of the bishop's treasurer was entirely remodelled in 1453-7 and in subsequent years; a new chamber was inserted over the serving place (Room 22) in 1466-7; the kitchens were repaired in 1474-5; and there is never-ending work on ovens, as if they too wore out with heavy use.

Throughout the fifteenth century, as in the fourteenth, Wolvesey was used as the royal residence in Winchester. Henry V met the French ambassadors there in June and July 1415 when they tried in vain to persuade him to abandon his claims and to put off the invasion which was to lead a few weeks later to Agincourt. The scene in *Henry V*, Act 1, is set (if anywhere, for it is a composite of long negotiations) in the great hall of Wolvesey, although the present of tennis-balls is an early and baseless rumour.

Henry VI's four visits to his uncle Beaufort in 1441-6 and his subsequent five visits to his friend Waynflete in 1447-52 were partly to inspect Winchester College, and partly in the course of other travels, as when he stayed a month at Wolvesey in June and July 1449 to attend parliament. For political reasons, Edward IV was an infrequent visitor, while Richard III seems to have been there in November 1483 during his moves to prevent the landings of Henry Tudor.

Wolvesey in decline
With the death of Waynflete in 1486, a change comes over our knowledge of Wolvesey. For a time this may be more imaginary than real, due to the loss of most of the Pipe Rolls for Courtenay (bishop, 1487-92) and Langton (bishop, 1493-1501), but the long episcopate of Richard Fox (bishop, 1501-28) is marked for the first time by rolls with a nil expenditure on the palace. The yearly average of expenditure in Fox's eighteen surviving rolls drops to only £2 8s 10d compared with between £20 and £30 a year for Wykeham, Beaufort and Waynflete, and over £18 for Courtenay. The method of account may have changed, work on Wolvesey being charged to the bishop's household or privy purse, but the charges which do appear on the rolls give no hint of this. Fox died at Wolvesey in 1528: in 1526-7 and 1527-8 there was some expenditure, as if for a short time the palace came back into more constant use at the end of his life (Period XIII). This expenditure continued under Wolsey (bishop, 1529-30),

The East Hall as excavated in 1970, looking south-east. This shows the tile floor, the square hearth, and (along the nearer wall) slots for setting up the great sideboards used in the marriage feast of Philip and Mary on 24 July 1554. (Copyright Winchester Excavations Committee)

although he never visited Winchester, and during the early years of Gardiner (bishop, 1531–51; 1553–55). Gardiner himself used Wolvesey in 1534–5, in 1547, and in 1548, years when he was 'permitted to retire to the country', but there can be no doubt that Wolvesey was now in decline.

The king of Castile was a guest at Wolvesey in 1506; Henry VIII visited Fox there several times in the 1520s; and Edward VI was at Wolvesey in September 1552 visiting Ponet (bishop, 1551–3) while Gardiner was in prison. The last great state occasion was in 1554 when Queen Mary stayed at Wolvesey for her marriage to Philip of Spain in the cathedral on 25 July. The queen's PRESENCE CHAMBER and gallery, where she first met Philip on the evening of 23 July, were in the West Hall, following a centuries-old tradition by which these rooms (over Rooms 39–41) were used by the monarch. The East Hall (Rooms 17 and 19), where Mary received Philip in state on 24 July and where the wedding banquet was held the next day, was transformed for the occasion with hangings of gold and silk and by the construction of a dais, great sideboards and a buffet (Period XIV).

For the next century Wolvesey was virtually abandoned. The bishops now resided normally at Farnham or Southwark and came rarely to Winchester, but Wolvesey was kept weather-tight and from time to time was intended for use. In 1603 the courts were removed from Westminster on account of the plague and were to be kept at Wolvesey, but at the last moment they were transferred to the Castle Hall in Winchester where the trial of Sir Walter Raleigh took place on 17 November. James Montagu (bishop, 1616–18), Lancelot Andrewes (bishop, 1619–26) and Richard Neile (bishop, 1628–32) all spent money on the palace, and in the early 1630s it was prepared for the reception of Charles I, but the visit never took place. In March 1635 Walter Curle (bishop, 1632–47) obtained instead a licence to demolish, but for some reason never acted upon it, and Wolvesey remained standing, its 'many huge and spacious roomes, vizt the Hall, Great Chamber, Galleries, Lodging Chambers, Chapell and Towers, all as voyd of Furniture as Entertainment', as a lieutenant noted that year in his relation of the western counties.

The palace continued throughout the Civil War, relatively untouched – contrary to local tradition – by Cromwell's forces. In 1660, when the episcopal houses were restored to the re-established see, Brian Duppa (bishop, 1660–2) began to repair Wolvesey and its chapel but most of the work was carried out by his successor, George Morley (bishop, 1662–84). Morley spent £1237 6s 1d on the old palace between 1662 and 1684, cleaning the moat, wainscotting the dining room, building a muniment house, and in 1671 wainscotting, paving and finishing the chapel at a cost of over £300. The palace at Bishop's Waltham, which

The south front, demolished in 1786, of the baroque palace, from the anonymous History and Antiquities of Winchester, *vol. i (1773). Drawn by William Cove*

Wolvesey Palace today: the surviving west wing of the baroque palace, looking north across the site of the demolished south front to the medieval chapel

was uninhabitable after the Commonwealth, was used to provide material for Morley's repairs. In the Hearth Tax returns of 1664 and 1665 the palace had twenty-three hearths, more than any other Winchester establishment apart from the College: Morley clearly made greater use of Wolvesey than his predecessors had done for over a century. But the inconvenience of the ancient building, the high cost of its maintenance, and the belief that Wolvesey would now continue in regular occupation by himself and his successors led Morley to take drastic action: in the early 1680s he replaced the medieval palace by a new residence in the BAROQUE style.

The baroque palace

Morley's new house, the west wing of which provides the present residence of the bishop of Winchester, lay around three sides of a courtyard immediately south of the medieval palace. The principal front faced south across the outer court, in which the medieval wool house, prison, gatehouse and other buildings still stood. The east and west wings ran

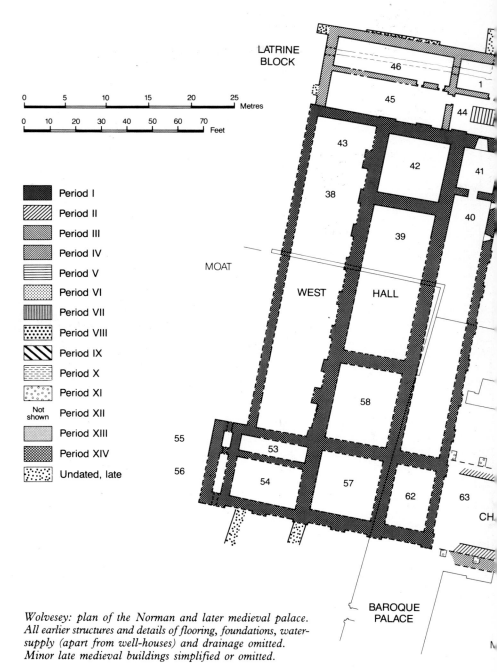

LATRINE BLOCK

MOAT

WEST HALL

BAROQUE PALACE

Period I
Period II
Period III
Period IV
Period V
Period VI
Period VII
Period VIII
Period IX
Period X
Period XI
Not shown   Period XII
Period XIII
Period XIV
Undated, late

0   5   10   15   20   25 Metres
0 10 20 30 40 50 60 70 Feet

*Wolvesey: plan of the Norman and later medieval palace.
All earlier structures and details of flooring, foundations, water-
supply (apart from well-houses) and drainage omitted.
Minor late medieval buildings simplified or omitted.*

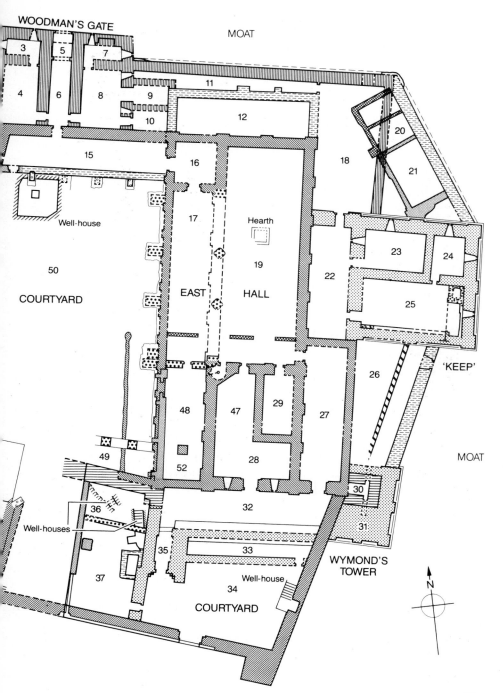

WOODMAN'S GATE

MOAT

3

5

7

4

6

8

9

10

11

12

15

16

17

Hearth

18

20

21

Well-house

19

50

COURTYARD

EAST

HALL

22

23

24

25

'KEEP'

26

MOAT

48

47

29

27

49

52

28

30

36

Well-houses

32

31

35

33

WYMOND'S
TOWER

37

34

Well-house

COURTYARD

N

The ruins of Wolvesey in 1757 by John Hadley, looking east across the courtyard towards the East Hall. A round-headed window from the original state of the East Hall, now lost, survives in the fragment of wall in the centre

back north across the filled-in moat to join the medieval palace, the chapel of which was retained in use at the north end of the west wing. The rest of the medieval palace was stripped to provide materials for the new building, which was designed by Sir Thomas Fitch (d.1689), and not, as local tradition based on a misleading quotation in *Parentalia* would have it, by Sir Christopher Wren. Fitch completed the south front before Morley's death in October 1684 and finished the west wing shortly afterwards, at a total cost of £2200. In his will the bishop left £500 to finish the house, but his legacy was not taken up until 1707–15 when Sir Jonathan Trelawney (bishop, 1707–21) built the east wing, converted the wool house into a coach house and stables, and, having demolished the old outer gatehouse, erected new gates and piers to beautify the entrance.

Trelawney's successors made no use of Wolvesey, however, so that by 1773 the house was almost totally neglected. John Milner, the Winchester historian, writing in 1798, regarded it in retrospect as 'the most perfect and elegant modern building of the city', but this had not deterred Brownlow North (bishop, 1781–1820) from demolishing all except the west wing in 1786, against considerable local opposition. The remaining wing became a white elephant, put to a variety of uses throughout the next century and a half, until in 1926 Theodore Woods (bishop 1923–32) proposed that it should again become the see house, in anticipation of the division of the diocese the following year. The necessary alterations were undertaken by the architect W D Caröe in 1927–8 and Bishop Woods returned to the palace of his predecessors in September 1928.

By the end of the eighteenth century the ruins of the medieval palace had reached very much the condition in which they are now, although from time to time they were

an ancient monument in 1915 and from 1921 to 1932 the Ecclesiastical Commissioners for England engaged W D Caröe to consolidate the walls, a task he undertook with great thoroughness, inserting the quoins and arches of red tile which are now so obvious a feature of the ruins. In 1961 the remains of the medieval palace, excluding the chapel, passed into the guardianship of the then Ministry of Works. The accessible parts of the medieval palace were excavated in 1963–71 and 1974 by the Winchester Excavations Committee on behalf of the Ministry. During and since that time the visible remains have been consolidated for permanent preservation and public display, and are now in the care of the Historic Buildings and Monuments Commission for England.

still robbed to provide stone for the repair of the various roads which the bishop was obliged to maintain. Nothing was done to preserve or investigate the ruins until the architect N C H Nisbett carried out some excavations and soundings in 1895–6. The ruins were scheduled as

Wymond's Tower and the east side of Wolvesey during consolidation works by the architect W D Caröe in June 1929

Description

Note: the greater part of the surviving structure of the medieval palace dates from the twelfth century. Later structures uncovered in excavation were, with few exceptions, domestic in character, such as ovens, ranges, and drains. These have mostly been removed so that the remains of the palace could be displayed as far as possible in their twelfth-century form.

Approaches

Throughout the Middle Ages, Wolvesey could be approached from the south, from outside the city walls, or from inside the city through the Water Gate to the east of the cathedral. The entry from the south, from College Street, is marked by a gateway on the line of the city wall which leads to the present palace in the surviving west wing of Bishop Morley's house of 1684. This gateway is on the site of the medieval gatehouse, demolished in 1715. It led into an outer court containing the bishop's prison, the wool house (converted into the present coach house in 1715) and the other buildings needed for the functioning of Wolvesey as the centre of the bishopric estates. An approach from this direction must have been possible in the time of Bishop Henry of Blois (1129–71), for the south front of his East Hall (Period III), the gateway in

the south wall of Courtyard 34 (Period V), and the gatehouse (Room 35) in the same courtyard (Period VI), all look in this direction. Even earlier the great tower at the south end of William Giffard's West Hall of *c.*1110 (Period I) seems to emphasise a possible southern approach.

But even if the bishop sometimes found it convenient to reach his palace directly from outside the city, through a gate controlled by his own household, rather than by routes controlled by the citizens or by the king, he nevertheless needed immediate access to his cathedral. The passage running east from the cathedral, through the Water Gate and along the south side of Wolvesey wall, is of great antiquity. It may have originated in the post-Roman centuries as a track which diverged from the line of the later High Street to run south east past the royal palace, between the Old and New Minsters, and thence east to the city wall. Whatever its origin, it served the bishops throughout the Middle Ages as their direct route to the cathedral and is probably the path along which Philip of Spain came first to visit Mary Tudor in July 1554.

The Anglo-Saxon palace of the bishops may have been approached only from the north, from inside the city. Like the later palace, it lay astride a north-south Roman street which survived in use as a field way through much of the Anglo-Saxon period. This field way may have been incorporated into the Anglo-Saxon street-plan of Winchester as a street leading south from Colebrook Street, and it is this now vanished street which may explain the location of Bishop Henry of Blois' great northern gatehouse of *c*.1158–71 later known as Woodman's Gate (Rooms 3–8, Period VII). Despite its size, which makes it appear on plan as the principal gate of the palace, Woodman's Gate served throughout the Middle Ages only as a POSTERN (*see Glossary*).

From the present entrance it is best to make for the great central courtyard (Courtyard 50), and to stand facing north towards Woodman's Gate (Rooms 3–8), with Giffard's West Hall (Rooms 38–43) to the left and Henry of Blois's East Hall (Rooms 16, 17, 19, etc) to the right.

West Hall

The greater part of the West Hall lies today outside the area in guardianship, below the bishop's private lawn and the northern part of the present house. However, the north end is uncovered to view and excavations in 1974 revealed the plan of much of the remainder. The West Hall, a residential block containing the bishop's private apartments, was built by Bishop Giffard about 1110, and was the first Norman addition to the Anglo-Saxon residence (Period I; see above, p.5). The structure consisted of a north-south residential block (Rooms 39–42, 57–8, 62–3) with a great tower to the south west (Rooms 53–6) and a walled garden in the angle between them ('Rooms' 38 and 43). Only the rooms on the east side, later known as cellars (Rooms 40–1, 62–3), were open at ground level; all the rest, together with the garden, were raised to first-floor level on a solid filling of chalk packed within the network of walls forming the substructure. The effect of this raised level can be seen today by comparing the level of Room 42 with that of Rooms 40–1, or with the interior of the range to the north, where the north face and PILASTER BUTTRESSES of Giffard's hall are well seen forming the south side of Room 45. This raising, which is also still reflected in the floor-level of the bishop's chapel (see below, p.30; not accessible to the public), was probably intended to give an imposing appearance to the building and to improve its outlook, rather than simply to raise the structure above the low-lying and rather damp floor of the valley: no other part of the whole complex was similarly treated.

The principal block, enhanced by pilaster buttresses on all four faces, comprised a high range containing the bishop's CHAMBER and great chamber (Rooms 42, 39 and 58), flanked to the east by a lower range containing the long chamber of the bishop's clerks (over the ground-floor 'cellars', Rooms 40–1, 62–3). These were the rooms which were occupied by royalty on their frequent visits: the northern chamber of the high range

(Room 42) was sometimes known as the queen's chamber and the garden to the west as the queen's garden, probably with reference to the visit of Queen Margaret in 1306. This garden, overlooked by the bishop's principal apartments and by the great tower, was itself raised above the surrounding terrain and looked out westward toward the cathedral. A similarly conscious integration of structure and landscape can be seen in other palaces of this period, for example in the bishop's palace at Beauvais or in the comtal palace of Henry of Blois' family at Troyes.

The great tower, on at least three floors, contained at its base the bishop's TREASURY and EXCHEQUER, with a private chapel above, and a high chamber at the top. These were all served by an elaborate system of latrines which were cleansed by the waters of a stream, later incorporated in the moat, which flowed along the west side of the structure, lapping the retaining wall of the garden. In the 1370s Bishop William of Wykeham completely remodelled this tower internally to provide a more secluded and comfortable set of private rooms (see above, p.18), and at the same time the treasury and exchequer were removed to some other part of the palace, perhaps to Woodman's Gate (see below, p.41).

Giffard's hall was built of flint and mortar cased with relatively finely-jointed blocks of diagonally-tooled Quarr stone from the Isle of Wight, the effect of which can best be seen from Room 45 or on the outside face of the east wall of Rooms 40 and 41.

The principal entrance to Giffard's block seems to have been through a vestibule over Room 41. This was perhaps reached originally by a wooden external stair on the site of Room 13, but Bishop Henry of Blois built a stone stair and porch (Rooms 13 and 14) at the north-east corner of the hall to provide a more fitting approach (Period III, c.1135–8). These works were carried out, as can still be seen, in a fine-grained, light yellow, oolitic limestone imported from Caen in Normandy, and were adorned with exceptionally rich carving (see illustration, p.8). This approach to the West Hall was later linked to the East Hall by a covered CLOISTER (Period X; Room 15).

Chapel

The chapel, at the south end of the West Hall, is the only part of the medieval palace which remains in use. Although it is not open to the public, it dominates the site of the ruined palace and was a crucial element in its development (see pp.9, 43–4). The present chapel was perhaps built by Henry, Cardinal Beaufort, in 1442–7 (Period XI; see p.19), but it stands on Norman foundations at the same first-floor level as the principal apartments from which it was entered. It was probably first constructed by Henry of Blois about 1130 (Period II) to replace the chapel of the Anglo-Saxon palace, the western apse of which can still be seen in the floor of Room 8. Henry of Blois' chapel, which was dedicated to

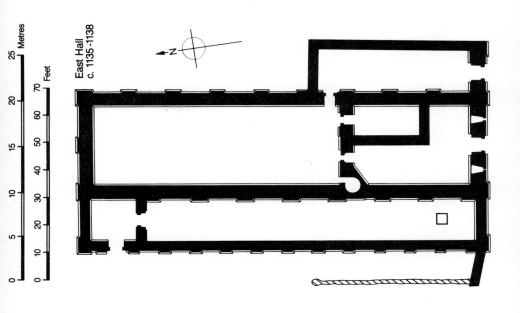

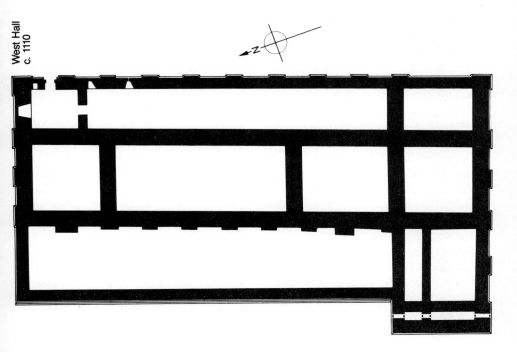

Comparative ground-floor plans of the West and East Halls

St Martin, probably lay like its successor at first-floor level, but below it there seems to have been a vaulted chamber, now filled in, which once perhaps formed a lower chapel.

The medieval chapel is roofed by a KING-POST roof of exceptional dimensions built of re-used medieval timbers and probably dating from the repairs of Bishop Duppa or Bishop Morley in the 1660s. The present paving and WAINSCOTTING are essentially the work of Bishop Morley (see above, p.22), but the chapel was repaired by Sir Thomas Jackson in 1907–9 and rather fully, if sympathetically, restored and altered by W D Caröe in 1927–8.

East Hall

Crossing the courtyard eastwards, or following the cloister walk (Room 15) from the West Hall, the visitor reaches the East Hall built by Henry of Blois in c.1135–8 (Period III). In its original form this comprised a great HALL (Room 19) rising the full height of the building, with a two-storey CHAMBER BLOCK of equal height to the south (Rooms 28–9 and 47). A GALLERY (later Rooms 17, 48 and 52) ran the full length of the west side, interrupted only for an integral porch to the north (Room 16). A similar gallery on the east side ran less than half the length of the building (Room 27). The walls of the central range (Rooms 19, 28–9 and 47) are considerably thicker than those of the flanking galleries, an indication that they carried a high roof which rose nave-like above lean-

Right: *Wolvesey in 1171, showing the East Hall with the 'keep' and Wymond's Tower to the right, courtyards and entrance tower in the foreground, Woodman's Gate behind, and the West Hall and chapel to the left. Reconstruction, looking north-east, by Terry Ball (HBMCE)*

to roofs on either side. Such an arrangement would have allowed CLERESTORY windows to light the great hall from the west and the first-floor room of the chamber block from both sides. Both the clerestory windows and the ordinary windows in the east wall of the hall (Room 19) would have alternated with a series of pilaster buttresses whose bases can be seen on both the east and west faces of the high range. The pilaster buttresses on the west side do not, however, march with those on the west face of the western gallery, the

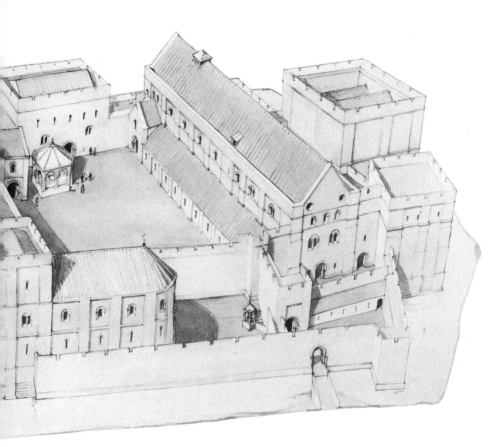

treatment of which must, therefore, although contemporary, have had a different rhythm to that of the high clerestory wall which rose above its roof. This was clearly the principal side of the hall: with long ranges of window ARCADES or arches at two levels in its pilaster-buttressed walls, it will have presented an impressive display when viewed from the bishop's apartments across the courtyard.

The relationship of the two buildings is emphasised by the entrance arrangements on the west side of the East Hall. Room 16 lay directly opposite the porch and entrance to the bishop's apartments in the West Hall (Rooms 13 and 14) and was later linked to them by a cloister walk. There was probably another entrance to the western gallery at its southern end, through what later became Room 52. This entrance was covered externally by a SPUR–WALL (later incorporated in the Period V wall forming the south side of Room 49) and by a long timber porch; inside the East Hall it may have reached a stair giving access from

Room 52 to the first floor of the chamber block.

The south front, as can be seen today from Courtyard 34, was symmetrically arranged with the high GABLE of the chamber block flanked by the end walls of the eastern and western galleries. The large pilaster buttresses of the high walls continued across the south front, as they did across the north. The former contained at ground level two entrances, both leading ultimately to the great hall. This front was designed to impress the visitor approaching from the south, as that to the west was arranged to delight those inhabiting the palace. The north and east sides were clearly of less importance: the outer walls of the eastern gallery had no pilaster buttresses, for example, and although the high walls, which could be seen from a distance, were fully buttressed, this side was certainly not originally treated with such elaboration as the west and south.

The first floor of the chamber block was reached from the hall by a spiral stair contained in a diagonally thickened wall at the north-west corner of Room 47. A passage in the thickness of the south wall of Room 27 led from the first-floor chamber into a latrine, originally presumably of wood, at the south-east corner of the building. The rest of the East Hall was built of flint and mortar on foundations of rammed chalk, laced with longitudinal timbers. Unlike the West Hall, which was entirely cased in ASHLAR (like the cathedral), the wall faces of the East Hall were of flint (presumably rendered and white-washed) with ashlar used throughout for QUOINS and JAMBS and for the CHAMFERED PLINTH which runs all along the base of the walls, inside and out, except along the north and east walls of Room 27.

Within twenty years at most of its original construction Henry of Blois remodelled the whole upper part of the great hall and chamber block, raising it by a storey throughout (Period VI, c.1141–54). The lower limit of this heightening is marked by a BULL-NOSED STRING-COURSE which can still be seen high on the south face, above Room 32, and on the north face, above Room 12, and which (because it is at exactly the same level at both ends of the block) can be presumed once to have been continuous around the high central range.

Above this string-course the north and east walls of the hall were widened to carry a gallery passage which ran in the thickness of the walls across the openings of the splendid ranges of arcaded windows which were now added on these sides. The necessary extra thickness at the north end of the hall was carried internally by a BLIND ARCADE of pointed arches set on CORBELS and decorated, like the round-headed gallery and window openings, with BALL-ORNAMENT. (The base and SHAFT of Purbeck Marble in the north-west angle were inserted c.1930 during the consolidation carried out by W D Caröe. The ABACI of Purbeck Marble in the north-west and north-east angles may, however, be original. The fine fourteenth-century carved head set as a corbel beneath the north-east abacus is a later, most probably medieval, insertion.) The wall-passage did not return south down the west wall of the great hall (Room 19), but seems rather to have opened on to a WALL-WALK over the north wall of Room 15. At the south end of the chamber block, where it can still be seen on the highest surviving masonry (above the south-east corner of Room 28), the passage turns east to run above the lower wall-passage towards Wymond's Tower and its latrines.

The top range of windows in the south face of the chamber block also belongs to this heightening, for the bull-nosed string-course can be seen running below them, but (pending unpicking and final consolidation of the high walls) it is not known whether this represents simply the heightening of the great first-floor chamber, or the addition of an extra floor; nor is it known how this level and its connecting passages were reached.

The great hall was remodelled again in the thirteenth century, probably by Bishop Peter des Roches about 1235 (Period VIII), but possibly by John of Pontoise (bishop, 1282–1304), for in 1554 a Spanish account of the wedding of Philip and Mary records that the great hall was called 'Poncia', which may be a corruption of 'Pontissara', the Latin form of Pontoise by which this bishop was known. The Norman great hall (Room 19) was now extended into the western gallery (Room 17) by the

Fourteenth-century carved head, inserted as a corbel below a twelfth-century Purbeck marble capital, at the north-east angle of the East Hall. (Conway Library, Courtauld Institute of Art)

insertion of an arcade of three BAYS on the line (and doubtless without the removal of the upper works) of the wall between them. At the same time buttresses were added to the west side of the block to take the thrust of the high roof and it can be assumed that this implies the reconstruction and refenestration of the west wall, which now formed the side wall of the great hall itself. The foundations of the inserted PIERS and RESPONDS and the corresponding buttresses can still be seen, as can the wall and doorway built across the former western gallery to form Room 48. The hall now resembled a medieval aisled hall (albeit of one aisle only) with the standard arrangement of BUTTERY (Room 48), passage (Room 47) and PANTRY (Room 29) at its southern end.

In 1441–2 the great hall was reroofed by Cardinal Beaufort (Period XI; see above, p.19). The rectangular shape of the great central window which was inserted at this time in the north gable of the hall can still be seen interrupting the main range of Norman windows. Its insertion also required the blocking of the small circular windows (now invisible) which had until then pierced the topmost level of the gable.

Early in the sixteenth century the passage (Room 15) between the two halls was remodelled and the west wall of the hall was rebuilt, at least at its south end (Room 48–52) where the new, thinner buttressed wall can be seen sitting off-centre on top of the thicker Norman wall of the former western gallery. The hall itself was refloored with plain glazed tiles, probably at the same time (Period XIII). Now too a wooden SCREENS PASSAGE was formed for the first time at its south end, leading from the courtyard across the three doorways to buttery, passage and pantry, and out into Room 27. The hall was thus in many ways of standard late medieval pattern when in 1554 it was provided with a great dais and other fittings for the marriage feast of Philip and Mary Tudor (Period XIV).

'Keep'

Leaving the great hall (Room 19), the visitor should pass through the serving place (Room 22) into the great kitchens (Rooms 23–5). Before the excavations of 1963–71 this square block had long been known as the 'KEEP' and was believed to be the 'very strong tower' (*turris fortissima*) put up by Henry of Blois about 1138. The excavations and study of the bishop's Pipe Rolls made this view untenable (see above, p.11), partly because all the evidence indicated that these rooms had always been kitchens and had never been known or used as anything else, and partly because, although undeniably and deliberately 'keep-like', at least from the exterior, the structure was in fact relatively weak, with walls half the thickness of contemporary defensive structures.

The north, east and south walls would have looked on to the moat when the 'keep' was first built. These walls are elaborately treated with central and CLASPING PILASTER BUTTRESSES, between which ashlar APRONS with multiple chamfers descend to ground level. The effect is impressive, as it was certainly meant to be, and is best seen at the south-west angle, just outside Room 27, or along the east face from the Pilgrim School playing fields. The window openings, arranged on up to three levels between each pair of pilaster buttresses, were narrow LOOPS and were clearly designed to give an external effect of several storeys and ready defence. In fact, there is no evidence that the building was of more than one storey internally, the three rooms rising open to the roof, which was composed of a pair of ridges with an east-west VALLEY over

The east front of Bishop Henry's palace, showing Wymond's Tower and the late medieval chapel to the left, the 'keep' to the right, and the cathedral in the distance between them

the internal SPINE-WALL. The roof gables were probably hidden by the external walls which would have risen to give a continuous and presumably CRENELLATED wall-walk (reached from the great hall gallery passage) around the top of the 'keep'.

The presence of large amounts of re-used stone, and notably of many round shafts, in the walls of the 'keep' (as seen from Room 22, for example) suggests that it was built after the destruction of the old royal palace in 1141 (see above, p.9) and should be attributed to Period VI (*c.*1141–54). Its internal arrangements were many times altered, as the ovens and ranges, traces of which can be

seen in several places, wore out and had to be replaced. The great hole in the south wall marks the position of the principal range, which was cut into the thickness of the wall, and the smaller hole in the west wall was perhaps similarly caused.

Returning to Room 22, which was used as a SERVING PLACE where food was readied for the hall, the visitor can see in the north wall, over the door, a deeply SPLAYED brick-lined window which was built in 1466–7 when an upper floor was inserted (Period XII). Brick was used at Wolvesey from 1441–2 onwards, mainly for ovens and fireplaces, but was never common in the palace.

Wymond's Tower

Passing south from the serving place into Room 27, the visitor sees to the left Courtyard 26 which was formed in 1372–3 (Period X) by the construction of a wall running diagonally south from the 'keep' to Wymond's Tower. This tower, which was originally named after the Norman hero Guiscard, began as a small GARDEROBE or latrine turret (Room 30) built in Period V (c.1141) to provide a permanent latrine at the south-east corner of the East Hall. The fabric of this early turret, which was afterwards encased in a much larger work, can still be seen from Rooms 26 and 27 where the later casing has fallen away. This enlargement was probably carried out at the same time as the construction of the 'keep' (Period VI, c.1141–54). It was designed to provide a defensive work of massive solidity, in the thickness of which the pit of a second garderobe was quite insignificant (Room 31). The full effect of Wymond's Tower can only be appreciated from the playing fields, where one can see how it forms with the 'keep' an imposing (if in reality a somewhat deceptive) defensive front. Unlike the 'keep', which is dressed partly with flint, the outer faces of Wymond's Tower are cased entirely in ashlar, with central and clasping pilaster buttrresses, between each pair of which a steep apron of eight chamfered courses descends to a plinth of at least two chamfered courses of larger size. Inserted corbels can be seen high up projecting from the south and east faces of the tower: these will have supported external wooden HOURDS or fighting platforms and may date from the time of one of the thirteenth-century sieges (see above, p.15).

The tower is solid up to second-floor level, apart from the two latrines. At this level, reached only by way of the upper wall passage from the East Hall, the tower contains a series of small vaulted chambers each giving on to a loop in the outer wall; a turning stair gave access to the next level which was presumably that of the battlements, from which the wooden hourds would also have been reached.

The bull-nosed string-course which marks the level from which the East Hall was heightened in Period VI also runs round the outer face of Wymond's Tower. This string-course and the access passage to the second floor of the tower demonstrate that the heightening of the hall and the massive strengthening of the tower are contemporary. The tower is likewise related in siting, projection, and external treatment to the 'keep', with which it is probably therefore also contemporary. These works transformed the east face of the palace and provided a strong defence around the East Hall, which was now raised so that it could both be seen and be lighted above the tops of the defensive works.

South range

The visitor may now return to Room 27 and leave by its south door to

The chamber block of the East Hall, looking south, with Wymond's Tower to the left

reach the interior of the south range. Here it is useful first to look back at the south face of the East Hall rising above Room 32, and at the east and south faces of Wymond's Tower to the right. From this point the relationship of the two structures can be seen and the line of the crucial bull-nosed string-course linking their fabrics can be traced.

The south face of the East Hall originally stood in isolation to greet the visitor approaching from the south. Soon after building the East Hall, Bishop Henry of Blois linked the West and East Halls by CURTAIN WALLS to north and south (Period IV, *c.*1138–41): the perimeter wall of the south range, with a small, square, ashlar-faced turret projecting from its south-east corner, belongs to this period. It incorporated a gateway to the south and a WELL-HOUSE in the thickness of its eastern side. Very shortly afterwards Bishop Henry divided the enclosed area south of the East Hall from the rest of the courtyard by building a massively thick and heavily buttressed wall running towards the West Hall on the line of the earlier spur-wall at the south-west angle of the East Hall (Period V, *c.*1141). This wall, which still forms the boundary between the central and the southern courtyards, incorporates a good deal of re-used stone, like the contemporary garderobe turret (Room 30) which forms the core of Wymond's Tower (see above, p.11).

A few years later (Period VI, *c.*1141–54) the bishop altered the

The south face of the East Hall, with Wymond's Tower to the right and Courtyard 34 with Gatehouse 35 in the foreground, during excavation. The bull-nosed moulding which links the reconstruction of Wymond's Tower to the heightening of the East Hall in Period VI (c.1141–54) can be seen running around the top level of the buildings. (Copyright Winchester Excavations Committee)

whole approach from the south by inserting a gatehouse (Room 35) into the previously open courtyard, and by constructing a range of buildings (Rooms 32 and 33) across the south face of the East Hall. The corbels which supported the frame of the lean-to roof of Room 32 can be seen inserted high on the south face of the East Hall. The construction of this high roof, which would previously have blocked out much of the light reaching the first floor of the chamber block, was only possible because Bishop Henry simultaneously heightened the East Hall, providing an upper row of windows in the south

front. The bishop's contemporary enlargement of Wymond's Tower was likewise integral to the construction and roofing of Room 32, for the west wall of the enlarged tower, which stands on top of the earlier east wall of the south range, shows the diagonal crease of the end of the lean-to roof of Room 32.

These works produced a strongly defensible entrance from the south: an attacker who broke his way through the gateway into Courtyard 34 would find himself under fire from several sides and forced to expose his right side as he turned left towards the inner gatehouse. If he took the gatehouse, there remained a long and difficult passage before he could finally gain the great hall or the central courtyard.

The southern courtyard was now greatly reduced (Courtyard 34) and separated by a cross-wall from a second courtyard (Courtyard 36–7) at the east end of the chapel. Both these areas were heavily used throughout the life of the palace and several buildings, all now removed, were set up in them from time to time. In the later fifteenth or sixteenth century (Period XIII) the present approach to the central courtyard was constructed immediately east of the chapel. The east side of the new entry was formed by a wall whose west face shows a chequer-pattern of flint and ashlar, typical of the period. This wall was founded on a series of RELIEVING ARCHES across the deep, centuries-old uncleared rubbish filling Courtyard 36–7, and may have formed one side of a building which then occupied the whole area of Courtyard 36–7, its east side resting against the west wall of Gatehouse 35.

During construction of the BAROQUE palace the structures inside the south range were levelled to form a yard, the perimeter walls being retained.

North range

Leaving the south range via Rooms 28 and 47, the visitor can cross the central courtyard, enter the north cloister (Room 15) and climb the stairs (Room 13) which would once have led to the bishop's apartments on the *piano nobile* of the West Hall. From here one can look down into the block which was added to the north end of the West Hall in c.1138–41 when Bishop Henry of Blois linked the western and eastern halls into a unified courtyard house (Period IV). This northern block seems to have been designed to serve at least in part as a common latrine (Room 46), the drain from which emptied through an arch in the west wall into the west moat, or ran east through Room 1 to pass through an arch in the north wall beside the gatehouse. The latrine probably served both the first and ground floors, being reached on the latter by steps down into Room 44 from Room 13 and thence via Room 45. In 1468–9 these rooms were filled with earth to combat rising damp and a new set of chambers was constructed over them (Period XII). All trace of these later structures was removed in excavation.

To the east a contemporary curtain wall ran from the latrine block to abut the north-west corner of the East Hall, thus closing the north side of the central courtyard (Period IV). After his return from exile in 1158 Bishop Henry used the space outside this wall to construct a gatehouse, later known as Woodman's Gate (Rooms 3–8; Period VII, c.1158–71). The gatehouse was reached by a drawbridge over the moat, the counterweight being housed in a stone-lined pit under the threshold, and the bridge raised by some mechanism over the gateway. The entrance arch is round, but the arch forming the vault over the northern end of the entrance passage is pointed. Since this latter arch is a structural and not merely a decorative feature, it confirms that the gatehouse dates from after the middle of the twelfth century. The vestibule (Room 5) was not vaulted, perhaps to allow an attacker to be assailed from above. The cut-back responds of another arch mark the division from the gate passage (Room 6), which in turn opens south into the cloister (Room 15). The arrangement to either side of the gate passage is identical, consisting of an outer chamber (Rooms 3 and 7), with loops commanding the front and flanks of the gatehouse, entered through a barred door from a large chamber (Rooms 4 and 8), the door of which could be barred against the gate passage. There were further rooms to west (Room 2) and east (Room 9). The latter was demolished in the fourteenth century, but the scar of its vault can be seen against the east face of the gatehouse, together with a stone-lined funnel which opens upwards into the first-floor chamber over Room 8. The function of Room 9, which could only be reached from Room 8, is obscure: it was clearly a place of strength, perhaps a store room or a cell.

The intended importance and military character of the gatehouse can be seen in its size, in its projection forward from the adjacent curtains, in the placing of loops to command both the curtains and the approach, in the devices to protect the entrance, and in the battered face of the adjacent curtain to the east. However, it never became the principal entrance to the palace (see above, p.13).

As a consequence of William of Wykeham's remodelling of the great tower at the south end of the West Hall in 1372–6 (Period X), the exchequer and the treasurer's lodgings seem to have been moved to Woodman's Gate. In 1453–7 and subsequent years the treasurer's house was entirely remodelled (Period XII). It was probably at this time that the walls between Rooms 2 and 4, 3 and 4, and 7 and 8 were removed and large windows and fireplaces inserted at first-floor level on all sides of the former gatehouse, whose ground-floor function as a mere POSTERN was now finally confirmed.

To the east of the gatehouse and contemporary with it (Period VII) a curtain wall was built to form a long, narrow, L-shaped courtyard which ended against the north side of the 'keep'. This courtyard could be entered from Room 8 or Room 22 and was originally open except for Room 9. In the later fourteenth century, probably in 1373–4, Room 9 was demolished and Room 12 was inserted as a winecellar conveniently placed at the north end of the great hall (Period X). At the same time, the courtyard was extended east to a new diagonal curtain matching that built south of the 'keep' in 1372–3. Against this wall during the next two centuries a series of bakehouses were built, rebuilt, and extended many times, Room 21 representing a late stage in this process (Period XIII).

Wolvesey as an early medieval palace

Wolvesey in the twelfth century was the very type of an early medieval palace on the grand scale. The three essential elements – hall, residence, and chapel – had been present since *c.*AD 1000 and probably from the time of Bishop Aethelwold (963–84), but it was the works of William Giffard and Henry of Blois between *c.*1110 and 1171 which made Wolvesey one of the great houses of its age. The exceptional character of the Norman palace consisted not only in the sheer size and quantity of its buildings, but also in their arrangement, and in the elaboration of their design.

Giffard's West Hall of *c.*1110 and Henry of Blois' East Hall of *c.*1135–8 were both huge for their date, but it is even more remarkable to find both on the same site. As far as we can tell, it would have been more usual to find a large hall (in the true sense) associated with one or more smaller residential buildings, or to find (as in many French and German palaces) these functions combined in a single structure.

The arrangement of the buildings at Wolvesey around a courtyard is the result not of single initiative but of a complex (if rapid) development. Nevertheless, the idea of a courtyard house is implicit from the moment when Henry of Blois laid out the East Hall in the mid-1130s. Although this idea may seem precocious in terms of secular domestic architecture, it would have been perfectly natural to Henry, whose home had for long been the cloister. The monastic plan may also be a key to understanding the scale and separation of functions seen in the buildings. But in this palace, erected by a man whose brothers were a king and a great count, it would be unwise to overlook the influence of contemporary royal and comptal palaces of which, especially in his native France, so little is yet known.

In the elaboration of their design, the buildings of Wolvesey were fully the equal of such palaces. Elaborate arcades of windows and other openings, such as those in the East Hall, were a basic element in European palace architecture of the eleventh and twelfth centuries. The arrangement of the chapel on two levels, probably with a lesser chapel beneath the main chapel, was another characteristic of contemporary palatial design. The provision of a great tower for the most private rooms and for the safe-keeping of treasure, the construction of an especially elaborate porch at the entrance to the principal apartments, these were further features which Wolvesey shared with the houses of the kings and other bishops of the age.

These elements were all present at

Wolvesey from St Giles' Hill, looking south-west towards Winchester College and across the Itchen Valley

Wolvesey by 1138 when the Winchester annalist recorded Bishop Henry's construction of 'a house like a palace'. In the years which followed the house was fortified 'like a castle' to meet the military and political needs of its owner, so that his legacy to his successors was both palace and fortress. And so it remained, repaired and renovated from time to time, until after another civil war, in which it played no role, it was finally replaced by a palace in the idiom of a new age, in the surviving part of which the bishop of Winchester still has his residence, a millenium since his predecessors first settled on 'Wulf's island'.

The bishops of Winchester

A select list indicating the building periods at Wolvesey assigned to them (for a complete list of the bishops, see F M Powicke and E B Fryde (ed.), *Handbook of British Chronology* (Royal Historical Society, London, 2nd ed. 1961), pp.257–60).

26. Aethelwold I, 963–84 (the Anglo-Saxon palace)
34. Walkelin, 1070–98
35. William Giffard, 1107–29 (Period I, *c.*1110)
36. Henry of Blois, 1129–71 (Period II, *c.*1130)
  (Period III, *c.*1135–8)
  (Period IV, *c.*1138–41)
  (Period V, *c.*1141)
  (Period VI, *c.*1141–54)
  (Period VII, *c.*1158–71)
39. Peter des Roches, 1205–38 (?Period VIII, *c.*1235)
44. John of Pontoise, 1282–1304 (Period VIII, late 13th cent.)
50. William Edendon, 1346–66 (Period IX, mid 14th cent.)
51. William of Wykeham, 1367–1404 (Period X, late 14th cent.)
52. Henry Beaufort, 1405–47 (Period XI, early to mid 15th cent.)
53. William Waynflete, 1447–86 (Period XII, mid to late 15th cent.)
54. Peter Courtenay, 1487–92 ⎤
55. Thomas Langton, 1493–1501 ⎟
56. Richard Fox, 1501–28 ⎬ (Period XIII, late 15th to early 16th cent.)
57. Thomas Wolsey, 1529–30 ⎦
58. Stephen Gardiner, 1531–51 ⎤
59. John Ponet, 1551–3 ⎬ (Period XIV, mid 16th cent.)
—   Stephen Gardiner (restored), 1553–5 ⎦
67. James Montagu, 1616–18
68. Lancelot Andrewes, 1619–26
69. Richard Neile, 1628–32
70. Walter Curle, 1632–47
71. Brian Duppa, 1660–2
72. George Morley, 1662–84
  (demolished the medieval palace; built the south and west wings of the baroque palace, *c.*1684)
74. Jonathan Trelawney, 1707–21
  (completed the baroque palace, 1707–15)

79. Brownlow North, 1781–1820
      (demolished the south and east wings of the baroque palace, 1786)
88. Frank Theodore Woods, 1923–32
      (restored and re-occupied the west wing of the baroque palace, 1927–8)
92. Falkner Allison, 1961–73
      (medieval palace taken into guardianship, 1961; excavated 1963–71, 1974)
93. John Taylor, 1974–84
      (consolidation of the remains of the medieval palace)
94. Colin James, 1985–
      (medieval palace opened to the public, 1986)

Further reading

The first serious investigation of Wolvesey was published by N C H Nisbett, 'Wolvesey Castle in the Twelfth Century', *Proceedings of the Hampshire Field Club*, 3 (1895) pp.207–24. Interim reports by Martin Biddle on the excavations of 1963–71 and 1974 appeared in *The Antiquaries Journal* 44 (1964)–50 (1970), 52 (1972) and 55 (1975). A reinterpretation of the history of the palace in the light of the excavations up to 1968 was by Martin Biddle, 'Wolvesey: the *domus quasi palatium* of Henry de Blois in Winchester', *Château Gaillard* iii (ed. A J Taylor, 1969), pp.28–36. Subsequent work in 1969–71 and 1974 led to a new interpretation of the twelfth-century palace (followed in this guide) which was first published in Martin Biddle (ed.), *Winchester in the Early Middle Ages* (Winchester Studies 1, Oxford, 1976), pp.323–8. The final report on the excavations will appear in Winchester Studies 6. ii (in preparation).

The only full-length study of Henry of Blois is Lena Voss, *Heinrich von Blois* (Berlin, 1932), but an illuminating character sketch is given by David Knowles, *The Episcopal Colleagues of Archbishop Thomas Becket* (Cambridge, 1951), pp.33–7.

For early medieval royal palaces in England, see H M Colvin (ed.), *The History of the King's Works* i, ii (London, 1963). The extensive continental literature can be followed in Jacques Gardelles, 'Les palais dans l'Europe occidentale chrétienne du Xe au XIIe siècle', *Cahiers de civilisation médiévale*, 19 (1976), pp.115–34.

Glossary

ABACUS (ABACI)	Upper element of a capital, often a square flat slab
APRON	Forward-sloping projection at the foot of a wall
ARCADE	A line of arches
ASHLAR	Squared block(s) of stone
BALL-ORNAMENT	Decoration consisting of relief-carved balls, either singly or in a series
BAROQUE	Style of architecture in Europe of the seventeenth and part of the eighteenth centuries, characterised by extensive ornamentation
BAY	A structural division of the length of a building
BLIND ARCADE	A line of arches on the face of a solid wall
BULL-NOSED	Word used to describe a half-round projecting moulding such as a string-course (q.v.)
BUTTERY	Place where liquor, especially ale, and other provisions are kept and issued
BUTTRESS	Support built against a wall
CHAMBER	Room, especially a bedroom, or room of some size or distinction
CHAMBER BLOCK	Block of building containing a number of chambers (q.v.)
CHAMFER	Surface formed when a square angle is cut away obliquely
CLASPING BUTTRESS	A support built at the corner of a building, against two adjacent wall faces
CLERESTORY	That part of a structure which rises above the level of an aisle roof, and contains windows to admit light to the central part of the building
CLOISTER	Four-sided enclosure, with a covered walk along each side
CORBEL	Projection jutting out from a wall to support weight
CRENELLATION	Battlement or indented parapet cosisting of alternating merlons (raised parts) and embrasures (indentations)
CULVERT	Channel or conduit carrying a pipe
CURTAIN (WALL)	Plain perimeter wall of a fortified place, connecting two towers, etc, and not normally supporting a roof
EXCHEQUER	Office charged with receipt of and accounting for revenue (see below, TREASURY)

FIELD	Open ground in front of a fortification
GABLE	Triangular upper part of wall at end of a ridged roof
GALLERY	Covered space for walking in, often open, partly open, or windowed on one side
GARDEROBE	Common euphemism for a latrine or privy
HALL	Large room for public business, also used for dining in common and by the servants for sleeping
HERRINGBONE	Zigzag arrangement of stones and/or tiles in a wall face
HOURDS	Protected wooden platforms projecting from the face or top of a curtain wall (q.v.) or tower to allow the defenders to command the face and foot of the wall
JAMB	Side post of a door, window, fireplace etc
KEEP	Fortified tower, the principal stronghold of a castle
KING-POST	Great post rising vertically from a tie-beam (q.v.) to support the ridge of a roof
LOOP	Narrow vertical opening in a wall for shooting or looking through, or to admit light or air
PANTRY	Place where bread and other provisions are kept and issued
PASTRY HOUSE	Place where pastry is made
PIANO NOBILE	Principal storey raised above ground-level, containing the reception rooms
PIER	Solid masonry support or pillar
PILASTER	Rectangular column, especially one of shallow projection, engaged in a wall
PLINTH	Projecting masonry, often chamfered (q.v.) or with decorative mouldings, at the base of a wall
POSTERN	Side or back door or entrance
PRESENCE CHAMBER	Room in which a great personage receives guests etc
QUOIN	Stone(s) forming internal or external angle of a room or building
RELIEVING ARCH	Arch inserted in or under a wall to relieve area below from weight and to concentrate weight as required
REREDORTER	Building containing latrines, usually flushed by a channel of running water
RESPOND	Half-column with capital and base where an arch or line of arches joins a wall
SALSARY	Place where sauces are prepared
SCREENS PASSAGE	Passage across the lower end of a hall (q.v.) separated from it by a permanent screen of wood or stone
SERVING PLACE	Room from which meals, etc are served